T0083061

Five Days that Changed the World

Bob Chilcott

for upper voices, SATB, piano, and optional timpani

Contents

1. Thursday 29 March 1455: The Invention of Printing 3
2. Friday 1 August 1834: The Abolition of Slavery 13
3. Monday 14 December 1903: The First Powered Flight 19
4. Friday 28 September 1928: The Discovery of Penicillin 29
5. Wednesday 12 April 1961: The First Man in Space 35

Timpani part 46

MUSIC DEPARTMENT

OXFORD
UNIVERSITY PRESS

Composer's note

I wrote this piece for the Worcester International Festival for Young Singers—the first festival of its kind in Britain. The theme of the festival was peace and unity, so I wanted to find an idea that would embrace this. The poet Charles Bennett came up with five new texts identifying events that have brought people together and, by their nature, become a force for good: the invention of printing, the abolition of slavery, the first powered flight, the discovery of penicillin, and the first man in space—all things that have changed our lives for the better. The dates are as precise as can be imagined, with the exception of the date for the invention of printing (29 March), which is Charles Bennett's birthday!

The piece is written for upper-voice choir and mixed voices, but it can be performed equally well by dividing the sopranos and altos in a larger choir. The timpani part is optional.

I would like to acknowledge the Catalonian composer Antoni Ros Marbà, whose work on a similar theme, commissioned by the Catalan Children's Choirs Federation, originally sparked the idea for this piece.

Duration: *c.*15 minutes

OXFORD
UNIVERSITY PRESS

Great Clarendon Street, Oxford OX2 6DP,
United Kingdom

© Oxford University Press 2013

Bob Chilcott has asserted his right under the Copyright, Designs and Patents Act, 1988, to be identified as the Composer of this Work

First published 2013

Impression: 12

All rights reserved. No part of this publication may be reproduced, stored in a retrieval system, or transmitted, in any form or by any means, without the prior permission in writing of Oxford University Press

Permission to perform this work in public (except in the course of divine worship) should normally be obtained from a local performing right licensing organization, unless the owner or the occupier of the premises being used already holds a licence from such an organization. Likewise, permission to make and exploit a recording of this work should be obtained from a local mechanical copyright licensing organization

Enquiries concerning reproduction outside the scope of the above should be directed to the Music Rights Department, Oxford University Press, at music.permissions.uk@oup.com or at the address above

ISBN 978-0-19-339008-9

Music origination by Enigma Music Production Services, Amersham, Bucks.
Printed in Great Britain on acid-free paper by Halstan & Co. Ltd, Amersham, Bucks.

Commissioned by Sing UK for the Worcester International Festival for Young Singers (WIFYS) 2013
through the kind support of The Bransford Trust

Five Days that Changed the World

1. Thursday 29 March 1455: The Invention of Printing

Charles Bennett (b. 1954)

BOB CHILCOTT

*See p. 46 for separate timpani part.

A programme note by Charles Bennett is available from the publisher's website.

Music © Oxford University Press 2013. Text © Charles Bennett. Reproduced by permission of the author.

Printed in Great Britain

OXFORD UNIVERSITY PRESS, MUSIC DEPARTMENT, GREAT CLARENDON STREET, OXFORD OX2 6DP

The Moral Rights of the Composer have been asserted. Photocopying this copyright material is ILLEGAL.

9
The quick brown fox, the quick brown fox, the quick brown fox jumps o - ver the la -
quick brown fox, the quick brown fox, the quick brown fox jumps o - ver the la - zy dog.
13
- zy dog.
unis. mp
mf
I saw them walk-ing like foot - prints in the snow.
17
T.
B.
unis. mp
Saw them walk-ing in - to hou - ses all o - ver the
mf
mp

21
S.
A.
mf
O-pen the door of the eye and let them
T.
B.
mf
world.
mf
tr
mf

25
mf
UPPER
VOICES
Quick brown fox, quick brown fox, quick brown fox, quick brown fox.
S.
A.
mf
in.
The
T.
B.
mf

29
quick brown fox, the quick brown fox, the quick brown fox jumps o - ver the la - zy dog.
The

mf
33
Quick brown fox, quick brown fox, quick brown fox, quick brown fox,
The quick brown fox, the quick brown fox, the quick brown fox jumps o - ver the la-
quick brown fox, the quick brown fox, the quick brown fox jumps o - ver the la - zy dog.

*pronounced 'zed'

45
Quick brown fox, quick brown fox.
mf
friend.
I watched them ga - ther to - ge - ther in - to
unis. mf
3
was ev - 'ry - one's friend.
mf
mf
49
f
Quick brown fox, quick brown fox, quick brown fox, quick brown fox.
f
words.
f
f
f

54
S.
A.
T.
B.
p
mp
I knew if I took the let - ters one by one,
f
p
f

59
p
mp
cresc.
knew if I held them tight in for - ty - two lines,
they could speak to ev - 'ry - one
p
mp
cresc.
mp
p
f
mp cresc.

64
mf cresc.
f cresc.
ff
con forza
ev - 'ry - where, speak to ev-'ry-one ev -'ry- where, speak to ev-'ry-one ev - 'ry - where.
The
mf cresc.
f cresc.
ff
con forza
mf
f
mf
mf cresc.
f cresc.
ff

70
quick brown fox, the quick brown fox, the quick brown fox jumps o - ver the la - zy dog.
The
f
con forza

ff
74
UPPER VOICES
Quick brown fox, quick brown fox, quick brown fox, quick brown fox,
S. A.
The quick brown fox, the quick brown fox, the quick brown fox jumps o - ver the la-
T. B.
quick brown fox, the quick brown fox, the quick brown fox jumps o - ver the la - zy dog.
mp
78
quick brown fox, quick brown fox, quick brown fox, quick brown fox.
- zy dog.
mp
mp

82
mf
Quick brown fox, quick brown fox.
unis. p
unis. mp
mf
The foot-prints of a fox
In the be gin-ning were foot-prints o-ver the page.
unis.
p
mf
p
mf
p
87
who jumps
in-to your eye and o-ver the la-zy dog.
mf
p
pp

2. *Friday 1 August 1834: The Abolition of Slavery*

Charles Bennett (b. 1954)

BOB CHILCOTT

Music © Oxford University Press 2013. Text © Charles Bennett. Reproduced by permission of the author. Photocopying this copyright material is ILLEGAL.

19
few words writ-ten in black ink on white pa - per can
mp dolce
words writ-ten in black ink on white, white pa - per can
mp dolce
words, a few words in black ink on white pa - per can
mp dolce
words in black ink on white pa - per can
mp dolce
23
cresc.
mf
set a na - tion free, can set a na - - tion free.
cresc.
mf
set a na - tion, set a na - tion free, a na - tion free.
cresc.
mf
set a na - tion free, can set, can set a na - - tion free.
cresc.
mf
set a na - tion free, can set a na - - tion free.
cresc.
mf
28

35
UPPER VOICES
mp
poco cresc.
One per - son, one good per - son,
S.
Some - times one per - son, one good per - son, can set a na - tion
A.
Some-times one per - son, one good per - son, can set, can
T.
Some-times one per - son, one good per - son, can set a na - tion
B.
Some - times one per - son, one good per - son, can set a
40
f
can set a na - tion, a na - tion free. A few
free, can set a na - tion free. Just a few words, a
mf
set a na - tion free, can set a na - tion free. Just a few, a few
free, can set, can set a na - tion free. Just a few words, a few
na - tion, set a na - tion free. Just a few, a few

45
mf
words on the o - pen page of the hu - man,
few words writ-ten on the o - pen page of the hu - man heart can
words writ-ten on the o - pen page of the hu - man heart can
words, a few words on the o - pen page of the hu - man heart can
words on the o - pen, o - pen page of the hu - man heart can
49
cresc.
f
hu - man heart can set a peo - - ple free.
set a peo - ple free, can set a peo - - ple free.
set a peo - ple, set a peo - ple free, a peo - ple free.
set a peo - ple free, can set, can set a peo - ple free.
set a peo - ple free, can set a peo - - ple free.

54
p dolce
59
S.
p dolce
Give me the good words. Make me the right per - son.
A.
p dolce
Give me the good, good words. The right per - son.
T.
p dolce
Give me the good, good words. Make me the right per - son. Give
B.
p dolce
Give me the good words. The right per - son.
63
mp
Give me a piece of pa - per to set me free. Pure words
mp
Give me a piece of pa - per to set me free, set me free. Pure
mp
me, give me a piece of pa - per to set me free. Pure words,
mp
Give me a piece of pa - per to set me free. Pure words
mp

68
mp
UPPER VOICES
Pure words on my o - pen, o - pen heart. A few
S.
writ - ten on my o - pen heart. Just a few words can
A.
words, pure words writ-ten on my o - pen heart. Just a few words can
T.
pure words writ-ten on my o - pen heart. Just a few words can
B.
writ - ten on my o - pen, o - pen heart. Just a few words can
poco rit.
più mosso rit.
73
p
words can set me free, set me free.
set me free, can set me free.
set me, set me free, set me free.
set me free, can set me free.
set me free, can set me free.
poco rit.
più mosso rit.

3. Monday 14 December 1903: The First Powered Flight

Charles Bennett (b. 1954)

BOB CHILCOTT

Music © Oxford University Press 2013. Text © Charles Bennett. Reproduced by permission of the author. Photocopying this copyright material is ILLEGAL.

5
learn to fly if you give it wings.
tr
7
mf
I said to Or - ville, 'Per -
mf
9
- haps.
May-be if per-haps we might
mf
mf
sim.

12
pos - si - bly try.
May - be if per - haps we might
14
pos - si - bly try.'
And we did.
And it was.
f
f
tr
mf
f
16
ff
Dif - fi - cult,
dif - fi - cult.
ff
f
6
ff

18
mf
Be - low us the ground was green and hea - vy with
mp
sub. f
mf

20
mf cresc.
sfz
mf
sfz
But a
fail - ure.
Rea - dy to break our fall.
mf cresc.
mf
mp
mf
sfz
f
mf
sfz
f

23
f
thought will fly some - times if you give it wings. I
f
mf cresc.

25
said to Wil - bur, 'Why not?' I said to Wil - bur, 'Why not, why
f

27
not?'
Most ev - 'ry -
f
29
- thing that could went wrong be - fore.
Most ev - 'ry -
sim.
31
- thing that could went wrong be - fore.

33
But it pulled us up in the
35
mf
end.
We said to each o - ther, 'Let's
mf
mf
sim.
38
toss for who goes first.'
We said to each o - ther, 'Let's toss for who goes first.'
And we

41
did. And it was. Glo - ri - ous,
43
glo - ri - ous.
We
sub.
45
T.
B.
car-ried it back to the top of Kill De-vil Hill.

47
S.
A.
T.
B.
mf cresc.
But we
mf
sfz
How ma - ny times? I for - get.
mf cresc.
mp
mf
mf
sfz
f

49
f
did and it was and it is and there you have it. Some-
f
mf cresc.

51
- times a dream will fly, some - times a dream will fly, will
f
53
fly, will fly, will fly.
ff
fff

4. Friday 28 September 1928: The Discovery of Penicillin

Charles Bennett (b. 1954) **BOB CHILCOTT**

Music © Oxford University Press 2013. Text © Charles Bennett. Reproduced by permission of the author. Photocopying this copyright material is ILLEGAL.

mp espress.
11
Some - times you find what you're look - ing for where you ne - ver thought it would
T.
B.
espress.
senza Ped.
14
p
be.
p
p
mp
(con Ped.)
18
p
Thrown a - way, near - ly thrown a - way.
leggiero
clet-tered the dish - es,
unis.
p
I clet-tered the dish - es,
p
senza Ped.

21
washed the pots.
cresc.
mp
washed the pots. I thought there was some - thing wrong but it turned out
cresc.
mp
23
legato
mp espress.
it turned out right.
Some - times where you ne - ver thought
right.
T.
B.
espress.
Ped.
senza Ped.
25
it would be there's what you've been look - ing for all a -

27
mp cresc.
- long.
Ho - li - day.
Just back from ho - li - day.
It was
mp cresc.
p
mp cresc.
(con Ped.)

31
S.
mf
meant to be. Se - ren - di - pi - ty. What went wrong had gone as right, as
A.
mf
meant to be. Se - ren - di - pi - ty. What went wrong had gone as right, as
T.
mf
meant to be. Se - ren - di - pi - ty. What went wrong had gone as right, as
B.
mf
meant to be. Se - ren - di - pi - ty. What went wrong had gone as right, as
mf

34
f appass.
right as rain. Some-times what you're look ing for will find you.
f appass.
right as rain. Some - times what you're look - ing for will find, will
f appass.
right as rain. What you're look ing, look-ing for will find you.
f appass.
right as rain. What you're look - ing for. Some -
f appass.
37
Some-times what seems wrong was right all a - long.
find you. Was right all a - long.
What seems wrong was right all, all a - long.
- times wrong was right all a - long.
Ped.
40
p

44
S.
A.
p
Green/ blue, it was green/_ blue. I hope_____ you find what you're
T.
B.
p
look - ing for. Hope
47
mp
look - ing for. Hope what you're look - ing for finds_ you,_____ hope
poco rit.
p
mp
poco rit.
3
mp
Ped.
50
più lento
what you're look - ing for finds____ you.
più lento
p
Ped.

5. Wednesday 12 April 1961: The First Man in Space

Charles Bennett (b. 1954) **BOB CHILCOTT**

Music © Oxford University Press 2013. Text © Charles Bennett. Reproduced by permission of the author. Photocopying this copyright material is ILLEGAL.

9
mp
They thought I might go mad, I might go mad. But I saw the
p
thought I might go mad, I might go mad. But I saw the face, the
(8)
mp
p
12
mp
face, the face of God.
mp
face of God.
mp
(8)
mp

16
UPPER VOICES
p
ah
S.
A.
p
ah
T. 1
mp
The son of a car-pen-ter cir - cling round the Earth. I saw how
T. 2
mp
The son of a car-pen-ter cir - cling round the Earth.
B. 1
mp
The son of a car-pen-ter cir - cling round the Earth. I saw how
B. 2
mp
The son of a car-pen-ter cir - cling round the Earth.

19
mp
ah
ah
mp
ah
ah
mf
beau - ti - ful our pla - net is.
A - pril twelfth, nine - teen
mf
I saw how beau - ti - ful our pla - net is.
A - pril twelfth,
mf
beau - ti - ful our pla - net is.
A - pril twelfth, nine - teen
mf
I saw how beau - ti - ful our pla - net is.
A - pril twelfth,
mf
mf

22
p
ah
p
ah
mp
six - ty one.
Stars are the al - pha- bet, the al-pha - bet of
mp
nine - teen six-ty one.
Stars are the al-pha- bet, the al - pha-bet of
mp
six - ty one.
Stars are the al - pha- bet, the al-pha - bet of
mp
nine - teen six-ty one.
Stars are the al-pha- bet, the al - pha-bet of
mp
mp

25
UPPER VOICES
S. A.
T. B.
mp
One hun-dred and eight mi-nutes, one
God.
28
hun-dred and eight mi-nutes. Can it be that you have come from out-er
cresc.

30
UPPER VOICES
mf
Keep
S. A.
mf
space? Well yes and I've seen some - thing beau - ti - ful.
T. B.
mf
mf
33
this beau - ty safe and let it
Keep this beau - ty safe and let it grow, let it grow.
mf
tr

35
UPPER VOICES
grow. Stars are the smile of God, of
S.
Stars are the smile of God. His face was the Earth look-ing
A.
Stars are the smile, the smile of God. His face was the
T.
Stars are the smile, the smile of God. His face was the Earth
B.
Stars are the smile of God. His face was the
38
God, of God.
back.
Five
Earth look - ing back.
Five
look - ing back, look - ing back.
Earth look - ing back.

41
UPPER VOICES
p
Five hun - dred and twen - ty peo - ple, five hun-dred and twen - ty peo - ple,
S. A.
hun - dred and twen - ty peo - ple, five hun - dred and twen - ty peo - ple
T. 1
p
Five hun - dred and twen - ty peo - ple, five hun-dred and twen - ty
T. 2
p
Five hun-dred and twen - ty peo - ple, five hun-dred and
B. 1
p
Five hun - dred and twen - ty peo - ple, five hun-dred and twen - ty
B. 2
p
Five hun-dred and twen - ty peo - ple, five hun-dred and

43
mp
have seen how beau - - ti - ful,
mp
peo - ple
have seen how beau - - ti - ful,
mp
twen - ty peo - ple,
beau - - ti - ful,
mp
peo - ple
have seen how beau - - ti - ful,
mp
twen - ty peo - ple,
beau - - ti - ful,
mp
mp

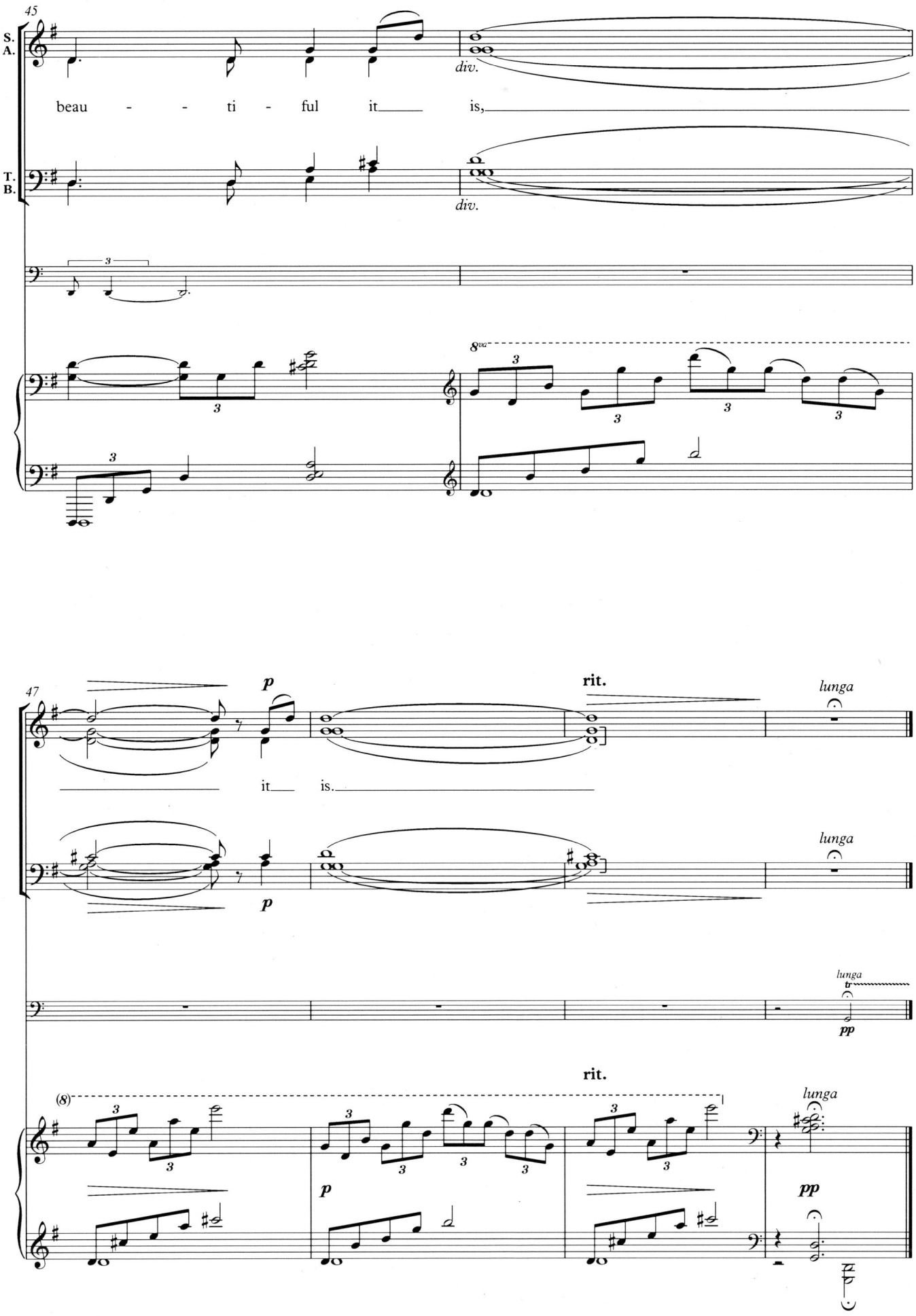
45
S.
A.
div.
beau - - ti - ful it is,
T.
B.
div.
8va
47
p
rit.
lunga
it is.
lunga
p
lunga
tr
pp
rit.
(8)
lunga
p
pp

Five Days that Changed the World

1. Thursday 29 March 1455: The Invention of Printing

BOB CHILCOTT

© Oxford University Press 2013. Photocopying this copyright material is ILLEGAL.

TIMPANI

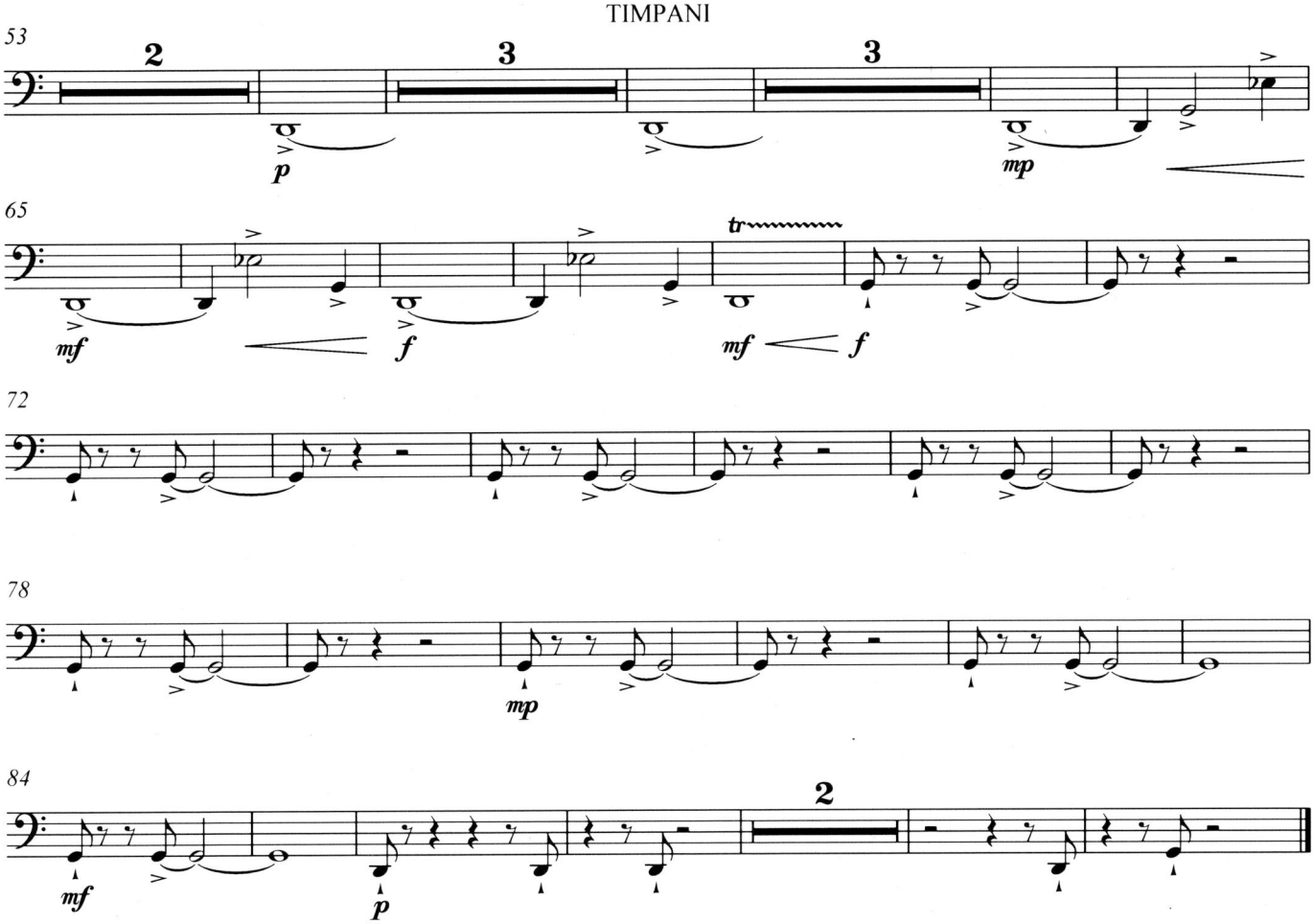

2. Friday 1 August 1834: The Abolition of Slavery – tacet

3. Monday 14 December 1903: The First Powered Flight

(time to turn)

4. Friday 28 September 1928: The Discovery of Penicillin – tacet

5. Wednesday 12 April 1961: The First Man in Space

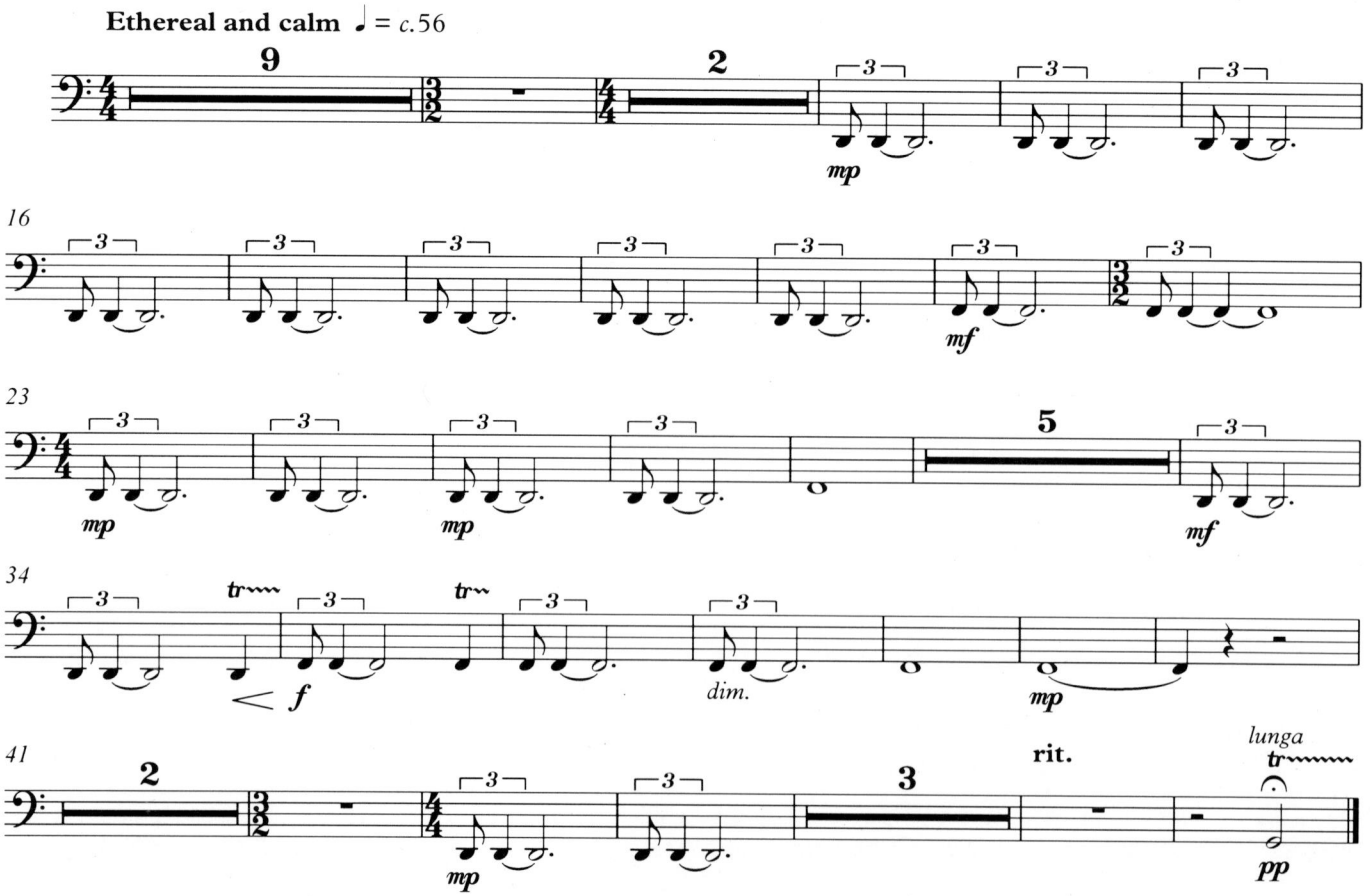

Processed in England by Enigma Music Production Services, Amersham, Bucks.
Printed in England by Halstan & Co. Ltd, Amersham, Bucks.